OCCASIONAL PAPERS SI

GW00731437

Reading the Signs: A *Qur'anic* Perspective on Thinking

Mohammad Hashim Kamali

International Institute of
Advanced Islamic Studies (IAIS) Malaysia

IIIT
LONDON · WASHINGTON

IIIT, P.O. BOX 669, HERNDON, VA 20172, USA www.iiit.org
P.O. BOX 126, RICHMOND, SURREY TW9 2UD, UK www.iiituk.com

P.O. BOX 12303, PEJABAT POS BESAR, 50774, KUALA LUMPUR, MALAYSIA
www.iais.org.my

ISBN 978-1-56564-986-6

Typsetting and Cover Design by Shiraz Khan
Printed in Malta by Gutenberg Press Ltd

Series Editors
DR. ANAS S. AL-SHAIKH-ALI
SHIRAZ KHAN

CONTENTS

FOREWORD

THE International Institute of Islamic Thought (IIIT) and the International Institute of Advanced Islamic Studies (IAIS) Malaysia have great pleasure in jointly presenting Occasional Paper 26 *Reading the Signs: A Qur'anic Perspective on Thinking* by renowned scholar and specialist in Islamic Law and Jurisprudence, Professor Mohammad Hashim Kamali. He has published widely on various Shariʿah topics. Many of his books including *Principles of Islamic Jurisprudence*; *Shariʿah Law: An Introduction*; and *A Textbook of Hadith Studies* are used as reference works in English speaking universities worldwide.

The paper advances a perspective on the Qur'anic conception of thinking, rationality, and critical reason. It begins with a discussion of the divine signs, the *āyāt*, and the prominent profile that they take in the Qur'anic conception of thinking. This being the principal theme that runs through the whole of this paper, other topics discussed include an identification of the sources of knowledge in the Qur'an, factors that impede rational thinking, and a historical sketch of the golden age of scientific creativity and its eventual decline. A brief section is also devoted to ijtihad and where it fits into the scheme of our analysis on thinking, followed by a short comparison of Islamic and Western philosophical perceptions of rationality.

Where dates are cited according to the Islamic calendar (hijrah) they are labelled AH. Otherwise they follow the Gregorian calendar and are labelled CE where necessary. Arabic words are italicised except for those which have entered common usage. Diacritical marks have been added only to those Arabic names not considered modern.

Since its establishment in 1981, the IIIT has served as a major center to facilitate serious scholarly efforts. Towards this end it has, over the decades, conducted numerous programs of research, seminars and conferences, as well as publishing scholarly works specialising in the social sciences and areas of theology, which to date number more than seven hundred titles in English and Arabic, many of which have been translated into other major languages.

Founded in 2008 in Kuala Lumpur, the International Institute of Advanced Islamic Studies (IAIS) Malaysia is an independent research institute, dedicated to objective academic research with practical policy-relevant implications on Islam and contemporary issues. In a relatively short period, IAIS has grown into a dynamic public forum that engages in seminars and publications of concern to Malaysia, the Muslim world, and Islam's engagement with other civilisations. IAIS Malaysia publishes a quarterly international peer-reviewed journal, *Islam and Civilisational Renewal* (ICR), a bi-monthly *IAIS Bulletin and Islam and Contemporary Issues*, books, monographs, and Occasional Paper Series. In the past nine years it has convened about 280 events, seminars, roundtables, national and international conferences on a wide range of topics of concern to Islam and the Muslim world. Details on IAIS Malaysia activities and publications can be found at www.iais.org.my. Professor Kamali's own website is www.hashimkamali.com.

IIIT LONDON OFFICE *and* IAIS MALAYSIA, KUALA LUMPUR
February 2018

READING THE SIGNS
A *Qur'anic* Perspective on Thinking*

The Qur'an teaches an essential doctrine of the *āyāt* (God's signs in the universe) which consists mainly of pointers to the providential purpose at all levels of creation. Thus it makes frequent references as *la-āyātin liqawmin yaʿqilūn* (*signs for a people who understand* God's *messages* in the Qur'an and who *exercise their intellect* i.e. 2:164). This evidential role of the Divine signs entails an accompanying demand placed upon humans to engage in a rational understanding of the *āyāt* and draw conclusions on the discovery of truth and correct guidance.

The human reception of the *āyāt* and any conclusions drawn from them thus depend ultimately upon the integrity of reason, without which humans would be incapable either of comprehending the signs or of responding to their message. The more abundant is an individual's native endowment of reason, the greater is the possibility for him or her to attain a larger magnitude of understanding and a higher level of response.

Sign reading is about decoding and unraveling of hints and hidden references in textual layouts and other cultural patchworks. It involves subjective interpretation and is ultimately a so-called 'process of semiosis' or meaning-making. What it tells us is that deeper meaning behind the apparent surface of reality is not only possible but rather necessary. Thus, the function of sign reading, or semiotics (also semiology), is to make us aware of our environment. It's about making us see beyond what it appears to be, and to look beyond the surface.[1]

---

* This is a revised and enhanced version of the article that appeared in *Islam and Science*, vol. 4, no. 2, (Winter 2006).

In nature, smoke is a sign of fire; heavy clouds are a sign of coming rain; fever is sign of underlying illness. Thus, although formally speaking, signs are classified twofold, conventional signs (human-made, cultural signs, artificial signs) and natural signs (naturally occurring signs), it so happens that the natural signs have historically and philosophically been downplayed. Natural signs are usually expressed and its patterns tackled through conventional signs and customary interpretations. The greatest part of our contemporary life, including science and technology, may be said to be built upon decoding of natural signs. By definition all communications are made possible through signs and only through signs. Yet, we treat the natural signs as some sort of raw material. Natural signs as 'signs' more often than not, fail our daily attention threshold. In the consumer trust of the day, it is less likely that attention will be paid at what something stands for or what it has to say. The higher the level of that trust, the lesser will be the attention to such messages.

In ancient Greece, signs were dealt with only in terms of 'medical symptoms' rather than as a worthy subject of philosophical inquiry. '*Semeon*' was the original Greek word for sign. It was Umberto Eco first to make a suggestion in his *A Theory of Semiotics* (1976) that despite ancient Greek sophistication in logic, grammar and rhetoric, they did not have a notion of general sign the way it is comprehensively understood today. Meanwhile, it is said that when Saint Augustine in the 4th century CE elevated the concept of signs within the domain of philosophical scrutiny, he left the natural signs out, promoting the conventional signs only. However it is suggested that in between the work of Saint Augustine and the 17th century there was an utter void in the field of semiotics of nature. Just like in almost any other discipline, the contributions of Islamic civilisation remain unaccounted for, either due to language barriers or because they are typically downplayed as irrelevant.

With the ushering in of the Enlightenment age, it is held that natural signs were finally preferred and promoted. Due to emphasised belief in reason and rationality, 'the natural' was valued over 'cultural'. With this, the human-made symbols were construed as unnatural or artificial. Again, this was a tendency of a more general cultural milieu drawing on unfolding scientific achievements of the day, rather than of semiotics as a formal discipline, which was still by and large limited to the conventional realm.[2]

In Islamic societies of the golden age, the cultural emphasis was more on natural signs, which in turn tipped over the opposite end of the scale. An obsession with the 'natural world' gave a lasting boost to all sorts of experimental sciences. This was due mainly to closer linkages the Qur'an sought to establish between the natural signs and the human intellect.

The Islamic notion of *ᶜaql* (intellect) embraces the faith dimension of knowledge that is also informed by ethical values. The prevailing reading of the Qur'an on rationality, which I present in the following pages, consists of a coalition of faith and reason which is also cognisant of the metaphysical aspect of reality and the limits therefore of human reason. Twentieth century Islamic discourse has shown awareness of that difference as it began to comprehend the subtleties inherent in the Western lexicon on rationality and its cultural overtones.[3]

I. THE DIVINE SIGNS (*Āyāt*)

The nexus between faith and reason thus constitutes the hallmark of intelligent Islamic spirituality, wherein human intellect and emotions are guided toward harmony with one another. The Qur'an repeatedly provokes its reciters to think about the signs of God in the universe and within themselves, to understand God's illustrious presence in them, and ultimately to vindicate the truth.

The word *āyah* and its plural *āyāt* occur in the Qur'an over 400 times, and even more so that the whole of the Qur'an introduces itself as a collection of *āyāt.* To quote the Qur'an: "We will soon show them Our signs (*āyātinā*) in the universe (*āfāq*) and in themselves (*anfusihim*) so that it becomes clear to them that this [revelation] is indeed the truth."[4] "And in the earth there are signs (*āyāt*) for those who seek certitude (*al-mūqinīn*) – as also within your own selves. Will you not then see?"[5]

God reveals the truth in a variety of ways, some explicit and others by allusion, the latter mainly through the modality of the *āyāt*, in order to provoke and engage the human intellect. The signs of God cannot be read just off the face of the signs but require thinking and reflection. This is indicated in the phrase "We will soon show them Our signs..." (41:53) which suggests that the signs may not be instantaneously visible to the naked eye. The whole concept of *āyāt* seeks to forge a dynamic relationship between revelation and reason: "(Here is) a Book which We have sent down unto thee, full of blessings, that they may mediate on its Signs, and that men of understanding may receive admonition."[6] A sign is also a portent and allusion to something other than itself and should not therefore be seen as the final message and purpose of the revelation containing it.

Approximately 750 verses, or nearly one-eighth of the Qur'an, exhort the readers to study nature, history, the Qur'an itself, and humanity at large. The text employs a range of expressions in its appeal to those who listen (*yasmaᶜūn*), those who think (*yatafakkarūn*), those who reflect (*yatadabbarūn*), those who observe (*yanẓurūn*), those who exercise their intellect (*yaᶜqilūn*), those who take heed and remember (*yatadhakkarūn*), those who ask questions (*yas'alūn*), those who develop an insight (*yatafaqqahūn*), and those who know (*yaᶜlamūn*).[7] These and their derivatives (mostly occurring in the active verbal form) consist essentially of open invocations and encouragement to thinking that is not limited by a methodology or framework. "*Afalā yatadabbarūn al-Qur'ān* (Will they not, then, ponder (*tadabbur*) over this Qur'an?)[8]" *Tadabbur* means concentrated and goal-oriented thinking provoked by the challenge to find something new or to solve a difficult problem.

To quote Netton (1989) on semiotics of nature, the Qur'an "may be described as a semiotician's paradise par excellence"[9]: "And how many Signs in the heavens and the earth do they pass by? Yet they turn (their faces) away from them!" (*Yūsuf*, 12:105). "And of His signs is your sleep by night and day and your seeking of His bounty. Indeed in that are signs for a people who listen" (*al-Rūm*, 30:23). "And the things on this earth which He has multiplied in varying colours (and qualities): verily in this is a sign for men who celebrate the praises of Allah (in gratitude)" (*al-Naḥl,* 16:13). In crowning nature as a sign-function of its Maker, and by explicitly including nature in the external world, as well as in human internal realities, the Qur'an virtually stretches the sign-spectrum towards infinity. So rich is the Qur'anic sign-weaved tapestry that the spectrum of phenomena qualified as signs is practically unbound to specific domains or categories. There is reference to signs as natural phenomena (*Yā Sīn*, 36:37; 36:33) as well as supernatural phenomena (*al-Shuʿarā'*, 26:4; *al-Isrā'* 17:59); signs as warning (17:59) and signs as blessing (*al-Naḥl*,16.11); signs as punishment (*al-Zukhruf*, 43:48) and signs as a feast of celebration (*al-Mā'idah*, 5:114); signs as tongues (*al-Rūm*, 30:22) and signs as text (*al-Naḥl*, 16:101), signs as historical events (*Yūnus*, 10:92, *al-ʿAnkabūt*, 29:15; *al-Naml*, 27:52; *al-Rūm*, 30:58) and signs in tangible objects (*al-Baqarah*, 2:248); signs as inherited knowledge (*al-Shuʿarā'*, 26:197) and signs as technology (*Yā Sīn*, 36:41); signs as evidence (*Yūnus*,10:15) and signs as human beings (*al-Anbiyā'*, 21:91; *al-Mu'minūn*, 23:50), to name a few. Without any enforced top-down framework, readers of the Qur'an were invited to wholly observe, travel, explore, experience, test, infer and each have their own unique way of interacting with signs.

Qur'anic references to thinking and the exercise of intellect occur in conjunction with basically five major themes: belief in the Oneness and munificence of God (*tawḥīd*); reflection on the Qur'an; man and the universe; historical precedent; and thinking itself. References to *ʿaql* (intellect) and its derivatives occur on 49 occasions in the text. The typical Qur'anic expression, *ulū al-albāb* (those who possess vision and understanding), and its synonym, *ulū al-nuhā* (people endowed with intellectual abilities) occur 33 times in the text.

Such expressions are frequently juxtaposed with the exposition of the *āyāt* themselves, such as in the verse "Thus doth Allah make clear His *āyāt* to you in order that ye may understand"[10] or in the verse "We have certainly made clear to you the signs (*āyāt*), if you will use reason."[11] Repeated references to pondering over the *āyāt* are variously nuanced such that they embrace within their fold the widest spectrum of people who may be endowed with different intellectual abilities and endowments.[12]

Al-Rāghib al-Iṣfahānī (d. 502/1108) defines thought (*al-fikr*) as the power of the mind that facilitates access to knowledge (*ᶜilm*). Thinking (*al-tafakkur*) is the movement of that power which is driven by the intellect (*al-ᶜaql*), and this can only occur when an initial image of the subject is attainable in the mind of the thinker. Thinking cannot therefore proceed over something of which no image exists in the mind. This can be said of the self of God, for example, as man has no image on which to focus his thought.[13] Man can only think over the attributes of God through the observation of His signs. Broadly speaking, thinking proceeds over the whole of the created universe without any exception; indeed, the Qur'an repeatedly invites such in respect to both the physical and abstract aspects of reality, both in the present and in regards to bygone history that is only perceived by the intellect rather than sense perception. Often the Qur'an gives examples, parables, and narratives of other nations, and then follows them with the reminder, usually addressed to the Prophet (ṢAAS)* to recount the narratives of the past so that the people may think and reflect over them.[14]

A hierarchy of five perceptive-cognitive functions is also suggested, including and extending through *samᶜ* (hearing), *baṣar* (sight), *fikr* (thinking), *dhikr* (remembrance), and *yaqīn* (certainty).[15] Given such a scale of intensified perceptive understanding, the Qur'an propounds the notion of *ulū al-albāb,* the thoughtful individuals who are possessed of proper understanding and response. *ᶜAql* is thus tied to the cognitive dimension of faith. Significantly, the very term for reason and intelligence in Arabic, *al-ᶜaql,* has at the core of its basic meaning the practical idea of "restraining" and "binding," that is, of holding one's self back from blameworthy conduct – being an interior self-imposed limit. Qur'an commentators understand thinking (*tafakkur, tafkīr*) as pondering and reflection, which is a mental activity and process, not an outcome.

* (ṢAAS) – *Ṣallā Allāhu ᶜalayhi wa sallam*: May the peace and blessings of God be upon him. Said whenever the name of the Prophet Muhammed is mentioned.

Tafakkur is considered as a form of *ʿibādah* (worship of God) if it is done with sincerity and good purpose. *ʿAql* in its Qur'anic conception is also one that conceives the truth, and it is always in search of it. This conception of *ʿaql* precludes one that is rigid, arrogant, and misleading. Some have also drawn the conclusion from the ubiquitous Qur'anic emphasis on thinking that all Muslims must strive to be thinking individuals.[16]

Al-Qaradawi has quoted Ibn Qayyim al-Jawziyyah's (d. 751/1350) views in support of his own observation to the effect that "thinking for an hour is better than worship of many years," and another statement that "thinking for an hour is superior to a whole night of prayer." To this Ibn Qayyim added that "thinking is the act of the heart whereas worship is the act of one's limbs, and the former is superior to the latter." The pious caliph ʿUmar ibn ʿAbd al-ʿAzīz (d. 101/718) is similarly quoted: "thinking over the bounties of God is the best form of worship". Abbas Mahmud al-Aqqad went so far as to say that "thinking – *al-tafkīr* – is an Islamic obligation. Just as God Most High ordered us to worship Him by performing prayer and fasting, He also ordered us to think in numerous verses and in so many different ways, all of which vindicate thinking as one of the cardinal messages of the Qur'an."[17]

The Qur'anic vision of knowledge may be characterised as knowledge that is founded in understanding (*fahm*) and insight (*tafaqquh*). This is indicated in the numerous references in the text which encourage rational observation, thought, and reflection on the observable world and the universe beyond. It is knowledge espoused with insight that the Qur'an has visualised in its expression *al-tafaqquh fī al-dīn,* that is, understanding the religion that signifies a rational and inquisitive approach to constructing a worldview of Islam. Islam, in other words, advises analytical knowledge and understanding that generate insight rather than a purely dogmatic approach. The two approaches are reflected in the familiar expressions *al-īmān al-tafṣīlī* (faith based on detailed analysis) as opposed to *al-īmān al-ijmālī* (undigested and uncomprehended faith). The former is preferred by common acknowledgement of the *ʿulamā'* of all the leading schools and *madhhabs*. Thus it is declared in a verse:

"Nor should the Believers all go forth together: if a contingent from every expedition remained behind, they could devote themselves to studies in religion (*li-yatafaqqahu fī al-dīn*), and admonish the people when they return to them,- that thus they (may learn) to guard themselves (against evil)."[18] We also note the distinction between thought-based knowledge and transmitted or received knowledge reflected in the twin juristic and hadith-related expressions of *ʿilm al-dirāyah,* that is, knowledge based on understanding, and *ʿilm al-riwāyah,* that is, report-based and transmitted knowledge. The former is based on understanding and insight (*dirāyah wa tafaqquh*) and takes priority over the latter. Whereas *ʿilm al-riwāyah* relies mainly on memory and retention, *ʿilm al-dirāyah* is based on cognition, understanding, and analysis. Thus, if there are hadith reports, or any factual reports for that matter, which do not stand to reason and understanding, they would be most likely discounted and abandoned, with the exception only of devotional matters (*ʿibādāt*) which are based on faith and submission more than on rational analysis.

Another feature of the Qur'anic vision of thinking is indicated in its emphasis on wisdom and good judgment (*ḥikmah*) which signifies the quality of thinking, its regard for values, and its outcome. Wisdom and good judgment can easily be said to be more important than technical know-how and expertise, as it can guide expert knowledge as to its proper application and the attainment of excellence.

The Qur'an mentions *ḥikmah* 20 times, and in about ten of these it is immediately preceded by the word *kitāb,* which is a reference to divine scripture – primarily the Qur'an, but also other divinely revealed scriptures. The text thus says with reference to Jesus that "And Allah will teach him the Book and Wisdom (*ḥikmah*), the Torah and the Gospel."[19] The juxtaposition of *kitāb* and *ḥikmah* is often contextualised by a reference to the sending of prophets who teach the people and guide them with scripture and wisdom (e.g., *wa yuʿallimuhum al-kitāba wa al-ḥikmata*) as it is said of the Prophet Muhammad[20]; the descendants of prophet Abraham[21] and of Luqmān.[22] The holistic, superior, and indivisible value of *ḥikmah* in the Qur'an is underscored in one of its verses to the effect that when God bestows wisdom on someone that person is indeed granted an immense source of goodness.[23] To mention *ḥikmah* together with the Book evidently means that the Qur'an should be read with wisdom and divorcing the one from the other by taking a totally dogmatic approach to the Qur'an goes against the divine purpose and intention of its revelation. To read the Qur'an in the light of *ḥikmah* thus means a comprehensive reading that reaches beyond the obvious meaning of its words to encapsulate the goal and purpose of its message and then also reflection on the ways and means of how its benefits can be realised for the individual and society.[24]

The repeated juxtaposition of the "Book and *ḥikmah*" in the Qur'an led some commentators, such as the Successor Qatādah ibn Diʿāmah al-Sadūsī (d. 118 H), Ibn Wahhāb, the disciple of Imam Mālik (d. 179/795), and the Imam al-Shāfiʿī (d. 205/820) himself to the somewhat unusual observation that "*ḥikmah*" is a reference to the Sunnah of the Prophet. Many have taken and followed this view; but since the text does not specify such a meaning for *ḥikmah,* the word should convey its natural and unqualified meaning as I have depicted in this presentation. Good judgment, insight, balance and avoidance of extremes, the ability to distinguish between truth and falsehood, and procedural accuracy are commonly associated with *ḥikmah* and *ḥikmah* as such becomes a dimension of evaluative thinking in its Qur'anic idiom. Besides, when the Qur'an declares that God Most High endowed the prophets David and Solomon and also the renowned sage Luqmān with *ḥikmah,* it could not have referred to the Sunnah of the Prophet Muhammad, as Sunnah as such did not exist in those times. The Qur'anic usage of *ḥikmah* reinforces the holistic quality of thinking; *ḥikmah* also seeks to forge a close tie between reason and emotion (*ʿaql wa qalb*) thereby encouraging what is now known as emotional intelligence. This is how the Qur'an and also the Sunnah often deliver their messages, for, unlike the modern statutory laws and texts, the Qur'anic guidance, commands, and prohibitions are often espoused with appeals to the heart and mind of their readers, often using the word *qalb* (lit. heart) as a venue of understanding.[25]

Al-Iṣfahānī defined *ḥikmah* as "the realisation of the truth through knowledge and intellect and it is manifested in the performance of benevolent deeds."[26] According to another definition, "wisdom signifies comprehension of the truth and reality and the ability to avoid corruption in one's quest to attain perfection."[27] *The Random House Dictionary of the English Language* similarly defines wisdom as "knowledge of what is true or right coupled with just judgment as to action." Wisdom is thinking informed by the light of the heart that often leads to action and contemplates its consequences in relationship with other relevant factors. This may strike a note with the renowned hadith in which it is declared that "fearing God is the pinnacle of wisdom (*ra'su al-ḥikmati makhāfatu Allāh*)"[28] It is presumably for this reason that the great religions of the world have urged the seekers of knowledge to combine it with wisdom. It is wisdom that confers a higher quality on thinking and helps knowledge to be used for the promotion of good, giving it meaning and direction.

In an effort to train the individual to enhance his or her quality of thinking, al-Ghazālī (d. 505/1111) discusses the two sources of knowledge that Muslim tradition has recognised. One of these is through human teaching and learning (*al-taᶜallum al-insānī*) and the other through divine teaching (*al-taᶜlīm al-rabbānī*). The former is externally transmitted from teacher to student, whereas the latter is conveyed by the Universal Intellect which is superior, more intense, and more effective than human teaching. This knowledge is internally acquired either through revelation (*waḥy*), which is a prerogative of the Prophets, or it is acquired through meditation, thinking, and reflection. Al-Ghazālī subscribes to the view that the essence of all knowledge is centred in the inner self of the human person in much the same way as growth potential that is vested in the soil and seed, and it is through teaching that the individual's potential is developed. These two aspects of knowledge, that is, the external and the internal, are complementary to one another. This is because no one can possibly teach or learn from any teacher all the sciences, some of which are learned through teaching but the rest inferred by the reflective thought of the individual. It is therefore important that the avenues of learning remain open both through teaching and through inner reflection, thinking, and illumination.[29] This is another way of saying that all knowledge is acquired and developed through the senses, inner reflection and thinking, both of which partake in natural endowment and development through external transmission and teaching.

Al-Ghazālī's views on the internal and external sources of knowledge tended to correspond with those of Ibn Sind (d. 428/1037), but which differed, at least partially, from those of the second/ninth century Ikhwān al-Ṣafā (c. 373/983). All knowledge, according to the latter, is acquired through the senses and none inheres in human nature. They maintain that knowledge developed through thought and reflection also originates in the senses.

The same analysis is extended to the axiomatic knowledge of postulates that are derived and confirmed through the senses. In support of this theory Ikhwān al-Ṣafā have cited the Qur'anic verse: "God brought you out of the wombs of your mothers while you knew nothing."[30] All knowledge is therefore acquired knowledge, a view which may strike a closer note with some of the modern theories on the subject.[31]

Islamic thought in the middle ages did not admit the ontological distinction between tangible entities that could be sensuously apprehended and entities of a spiritual or subliminal nature. This may be said to be a more sound and realistic view of reality than is allowed for by the modern positivist doctrines of science. Being is manifested at various levels and in several forms, none of which is less real than the other. Arabic thought employed the notions systematised in Stoic theory that divide being into three locations: verbal utterance, psychic representation, and reality – without this last in any sense having exclusive title to Being. Abū Naṣr al-Fārābī (d. 950 CE) took up this view and assimilated psychic representation to the entities of reason. Others rehearsed this division with the addition of a fourth location, that of Scripture. Reality thus had a four-fold manifestation, depending on whether the subject existed immediately in itself or whether its like was graven in the mind (*dhihn,* psyche) composed of sounds, which together indicates the psychic representation, or was manifested in characters standing for sound and speech. All four have a basic characteristic in common which is existence (*wujūd, ḥaqīqah*).[32]

The Islamic and Western perceptions of creative and evaluative thinking both recognise this to be a skill that is developed through training and controlled exercise. It is through training and thinking that we adopt new patterns of perceiving reality which we are able to see differently and creatively. It is generally acceded that creative thinking and critical thinking go hand-in-hand and complement one another. Critical thinking means "involving or exercising skilled judgment or observation." Thinking is critical when it evaluates the reasoning behind a decision. Such evaluation must, however, be carried forth in a constructive manner.[33] The purpose of critical thinking is to achieve understanding, evaluate viewpoints, and solve problems. In general, one's thinking is likely to become critical when concrete learning experiences precede abstract thought.[34] This strikes a parallel note, in its Islamic idiom, with thinking that is espoused with *ḥikmah*.

The famous yet controverted hadith "The first (being) God created is the intelligence (*awwalu mā khalaqa Allāhu al-ʿaqla*)" sparked prolonged discussions among Muslim thinkers over many centuries over the implications of this statement. Among the issues debated was the priority of reason over revelation and the respective role of each in their mutual inter-dependence. Another issue was whether the disparity among humans in respect of reason also affected the modalities of moral obligation. Some prominent thinkers including Abū Bakr al-Rāzī (d. 313/925) apparently advocated the primacy of reason over the revelation. This would be properly known as "rationalism," which deems the primacy of reason over revelation. This is different from "rationality" which means treating any issue by using reason without giving reason priority.

II. SOURCES AND INSTRUMENTS OF KNOWLEDGE

Commenting on the Qur'anic passage quoted earlier, Muhammad Iqbal observed that the Qur'an regards both *anfus* (self) and *āfāq* (world) as sources of knowledge. God reveals His signs in inner as well as outer experience. The Qur'an thus opens fresh vistas of knowledge in the domain of man's inner experience. Mystic experience and intuition, then, however unusual and abnormal, must now be regarded as perfectly natural and open to scrutiny like other aspects of human experience.[35] But inner experience is only one source of human knowledge. The outer experience in the Qur'an, Iqbal continues on the same page, unfolds two other sources of knowledge – nature and history, and it is in tapping these sources of knowledge that "the spirit of Islam is seen at its best."

The Qur'an sees the signs of reality in the sun, the moon, the alternation of day and night, the perpetual changes of the winds, the variety of human colors and tongues, and in fact in the whole of nature as revealed to the sense-perception of man. The Muslim's duty is to reflect on these signs and not to pass by them *as if he is deaf and blind* (cf. *al-Aʿrāf,* 7:179), for he who does not see these signs in this life will remain blind to the realities of the life to come. The divine signs are observed through sense-perception using mainly the faculties of hearing, sight, and intellect: "Do they not travel through the land, so that their hearts (and minds) may thus learn wisdom ?"[36] The emphasis in this verse is on the faculty of reason and understanding, suggesting that not all of our information about nature comes directly from sensation, for if that were the case we would be no different from animals.

Frequent references to sense-perception as the principal mode of receiving the *āyāt* show the scientific/experimental import of the Qur'an. The Qur'an goes even further to suggest sense perception as the only avenue of knowledge, as the text already reviewed provides: "And Allah brought you forth from the wombs of your mothers knowing nothing, and gave you hearing and sight and hearts that haply ye might give thanks."[37]

Knowledge of the signs is therefore acquired through the use of these faculties. In another verse, the Qur'an praises "those who listen to the Word, and follow the best (meaning) in it)."[38] This verse apparently subjects the data of sense-perception to the exercise of intellectual selection. The text also teaches that sense-perception does not perceive all reality: "But nay! I swear by that which you see, and that which you do not see."[39] Certainty (*yaqīn*) may also be beyond the reach of human intellect, as the human mind may be blurred by the variables of time and space. What is deemed certain today may be uncertain tomorrow.

We also note that according to the teachings of the Qur'an, the universe is dynamic in its origin, finite, and capable of increase. Early Muslim thinkers do not seem to have grasped the Qur'anic emphasis on inductive reasoning and experimentation. It was indeed a slow realisation for Muslim thinkers to note "that the spirit of the Qur'an was essentially anti-classical." Putting full confidence in Greek reasoning, Muslim thinkers tried to understand the Qur'an in the light of Greek philosophy, which in the beginning of their careers they had studied with so much enthusiasm.

The substance of Iqbal's analysis on this subject is also upheld by Malek Bennabi (1905-1973), who understands the creative impulse of the Qur'an as the motivating force behind the efflorescence of science at a time when Muslim thinkers began to grasp the full impact of the Qur'an on experimentation and inductive reasoning.[40]

The dynamic conception of the universe in the Qur'an is also seen by its conception of life as an evolutionary movement in time. History thus constitutes the third source of knowledge in the Qur'an. It is one of the most essential teachings of the Qur'an, as Iqbal has further observed, that nations are collectively judged, and suffer for their misdeeds here and now. The Qur'an thus constantly cites historical instances, and urges upon the reader to reflect on the past and present experiences of mankind:

> Many were the Ways of Life that have passed away before you: travel through the earth, and see what was the end of those who rejected Truth![41]
> If a wound hath touched you, be sure a similar wound hath touched the others. Such days (of varying fortunes) We give to men and men by turns.[42]
> Of those We have created are people who direct (others) with truth. And dispense justice therewith. Those who reject Our signs, We shall gradually visit with punishment, in ways they perceive not; Respite will I grant unto them: for My scheme is strong (and unfailing).[43]

The Qur'an's interest in history as a source of human knowledge extends farther than mere indication of historical generalisations. "It has given us one of the most fundamental principles of historical criticism."[44] Since accuracy in recording facts is an indispensable condition of history as a science, accuracy depends ultimately on those who report them. The reporter's personal character is thus an important factor in judging his testimony. The Qur'an says "O ye who believe! If a wicked person comes to you with any news, ascertain the truth."[45] It is the application of the principle embodied in this verse to the reporters of the Prophet's traditions out of which were gradually evolved the canons of historical criticism.

A scientific treatment of history, however, requires a wider experience, a greater maturity of practical reason, and a fuller realisation of certain basic ideas regarding the nature of life and time. These are in the main three, and taken together they constitute the foundation of Qur'anic teaching.

(1) **The unity of human origin**: The Qur'an states: "He created you (all) from a single person."[46] But the perception of life as an organic unity is a slow achievement. Islam sowed the germ of this aspiration and it became a Qur'anic assignment of man to work towards its realisation. Notwithstanding the fact that Christianity, long before Islam, brought the message of equality to mankind, the Roman Empire had no more than a general and abstract conception of human unity. On the other hand, the growth of territorial nationalism in Europe has tended to stifle the broad human element in the art and literature of Europe. Colonialism was also inspired by a self-image of superiority.[47] It was quite otherwise with Islam. The impulse of Islam was from the outset to make the idea of human unity a living factor in the Muslim experience that was to be taken towards fuller fruition.

(2) **A keen sense of the reality of time, and the concept of life as a continuous movement in time**: The Qur'anic view of the alternation of day and night as a sign of the ultimate Reality which appears in a fresh glory every moment and the tendency in Muslim metaphysics to regard time as objective – all this constituted the intellectual heritage and ideals of Islam.

(3) **The merger between religious and secular values**: This is a unique feature of Islamic thought which is distinguished by its attempt to bring harmony between them, probably for the first time in history. It was in the state of Madinah that we encounter a clear example where universally proclaimed moral values formed the criteria of political judgment. Political leaders and statesmen were expected to recognise not only the value of efficiency, but also of justice, human dignity, equality, and freedom. In his renowned *Philosophy of History,* Hegel (1770-1831) recognised that the unity between the secular and the spiritual took place in Islamic society and civilisation long before it made any impact in the modern West:

> We must therefore regard [the reconciliation between the secular and spiritual] as commencing rather in the enormous contrast between the spiritual religious principles, and the barbarian Real World. For spirit as the consciousness of an inner world is, at the commencement, itself still in the abstract form. All that is secular is consequently given over to rudeness and capricious violence. The Mohammedan principle, the enlightenment of the oriental world, is the first to contravene this barbarism and caprice. We find it developing itself later and more rapidly than Christianity; for the latter needed eight centuries to grow into a political form.[48]

The modern West followed the example of the historical Islamic world in demanding that holders of political power operate under a set of moral rules. But as the modern West harmonised the secular and religious only nationally, the international realm was free to operate under the dynamics of power politics and secular rudeness. This failure was a cause of the senseless violence that claimed over 100 million war victims in the twentieth century. Recognition of the danger of the purely secular politics led to the creation of the United Nations.

Safi has rightly noted the irony that contemporary Muslim societies have unfortunately followed a similar course in decoupling the secular and the religious and now find themselves entangled in a crisis of legitimacy. Many Muslim regimes are driven by the logic of power and operate outside the realm of moral correctness. It is alarming to see that this de-coupling has impacted the religiously inspired movements, which seem to succumb to the logic of power in their readiness to employ amoral – even immoral – strategies in their fight against political corruption and oppression.[49]

III. OBSTACLES TO CORRECT REASONING

The Qur'anic emphasis on pondering over the *āyāt* is also underscored by a set of guidelines to ensure a correct outcome of reflection and thinking over them. The text thus draws attention to a series of exclusions and factors that stand in the way of the proper functioning of intellect:

(1) Pursuit of caprice (*hawā*) which may consist of love, hatred, pomposity and prejudice that confound impartiality and sound judgment: "Have you seen the (predicament of) one who took as his god his own vain desire (*hawā*) and God left him to stray?"[50] "And if you follow their desires after the knowledge has come to you, you shall have no guardian or helper in God."[51] The choice is between two alternatives: caprice (*hawā*) and guidance (*hudā*); the former evidently obfuscates one's attempt to attain the latter.

(2) Pursuit of conjecture in the face of certitude: "And surely conjecture (*al-Ẓann*) avails nothing against the truth (*al-Ḥaqq*)."[52] "And take not a position on that of which you have no knowledge (*ʿIlm*), surely the hearing, the sight and the heart are all accountable."[53] Knowledge and truth stand in contradistinction with the pursuit of *Ẓann*. Note that the text says one should not follow *Ẓann* until it is established and elevated to the rank of *ʿIlm*. It does not say that one should avoid *Ẓann* altogether. In another place, *Ẓann* occurs side by side with *hawā* or that "which they themselves desire."[54] This is the kind of *Ẓann* that is meant. Knowledge is established by sense-perception that often begins with a measure of speculation and doubt but which is affirmed by the light of reason and conviction. Some commentators maintain that the main context for this guideline is religion: thus it is said that one should not take speculative positions in matters of belief. As for scientific enquiry and pursuit of knowledge, *Ẓann* is neither discouraged nor avoidable.[55]

The ultimate purpose of this engagement is to attain the truth. Once the truth is attained, one should then commit oneself to it and observe it: "Then what is there beyond the truth – except misguidance?"[56] "And the word of thy Lord ends with truth and with justice. There shall be no change to His words."[57]

(3) Blind imitation of others: The correct exercise of reason in Islam is tied to personal conviction as opposed to indiscriminate following of others, hallowed custom, and precedent. These must be judged in the light of reason and abandoned if found deviant and misleading: The misguided will say, as the Qur'an provides: "'Nay! we shall follow the ways of our fathers.' What! even though their fathers were void of wisdom and guidance?"[58] This was the response that prophet Abraham and other great prophets received from their detractors, but the text address them again and again that "Indeed, you and your forefathers have obviously gone astray!"[59] As we shall presently elaborate, indiscriminate imitation of others is widely held to be the single most damaging cause of the decline of creative thinking among Muslims.

(4) Oppressive Dictatorship: The Qur'an takes to task arrogant dictators and those who support them and follow them. Hence the plea of those who say "O our Sustainer! Behold, we paid heed unto our leaders and our great men, and it is they who have led us astray from the right path!"[60] should be of no merit. In a number of other places the text denounces the Pharaoh and Qārūn for their oppressive ways who misled their people in rejecting the guidance that was conveyed to them.[61]

IV. DECLINE OF CRITICAL THINKING

I shall not retrace well-documented history that Muslim thinkers were pioneers in the creation of new knowledge. It was due to the impact of the Qur'an that, in contrast to the Greeks who excelled in deductive method of reasoning and logic, Muslim scientists distinguished themselves in inductive and experimental approaches to scientific enquiry. The Qur'an's repeated invocations to truth discovery, to acquisition of knowledge, and investigation of the observable world provided moral and spiritual incentives to scientific creativity. The golden age of Muslim science started around 700 CE and lasted until about 1350 CE. Great thinkers such as Ibn Sīnā, Jābir ibn Ḥayyān, Abū Bakr Zakarriyā al-Rāzī, Abū Rayḥān al-Bayrūnī, Ibn al-Nafīs al-Dimashqī, al-Khawārizmī, and many others have left a rich legacy of contributions to the advancement of sciences in anatomy, medicine, mathematics, astronomy, chemistry, optics, etc.[62] Amid Muslim societies of their times, the linguistic and other human-made signs and symbols in formalised languages of sciences, textual analysis, architecture or art forms were anything but neglected. A highly sophisticated literary culture and book industry boomed to an unprecedented scale.[63] In popular imagination, the ink of learned people was regarded as sacred and the pen was seen as the first thing to have been created by God. So it is hard to say, for instance, which of the signs in that era, the human-made or the naturally occurring signs, got the better attention. Culture and nature in a healthy symbiotic relationship was reflected, for example, in the nature-friendly Islamic architecture of the time.[64]

After the fourteenth century creative thinking began to decline in the Islamic world due to a variety of factors, including the Mongol invasion and burning of Baghdad, the defeat of the Muslim Arabs in Spain and the continuing crusades, the collapse of the Ottoman caliphate, and the ensuing onslaught of colonialism. The creative impulse of Islamic thought suffered setbacks as a result. Muslims were also beset with many internal problems including the alienation of philosophers, scientists, and thinkers from the theologians, sectarian controversies, and the prevalence of intellectual conservatism and *taqlīd* (imitation of past authority). Philosophy and the sciences fell into a rapid decline while more rigid forms of instruction and narrower curricula prevailed. It was argued that orthodoxy was being threatened and that there was a need to restrain thinkers in order to defend religion. The latitude and diversity of discourse that expanded the scope of religious sciences, *kalām, tafsīr,* hadith, and fiqh gave way to narrower criteria of *kufr, bidʿah,* and *taqlīd* and the so-called closing of the door of ijtihad (*sadd bāb al-ijtihād*).[65]

More recently, a certain abuse of Islamic authority operated by a dogmatic radicalism has exacerbated the decline of creative thought among Muslims. The situation is not helped by the prevalence of passivity in popular culture concerning the dogmatic excesses of these ardent proponents of *taqlīd*. One of the salient features of this mindset is a certain ignorance of the essential impulse of the Qur'an on creative thought. Malek Bennabi put it succinctly that the crisis of a civilisation and a society at a critical point of its history "is not the paucity of its material objects but the poverty of its ideas."[66]

V. WHAT OF IJTIHAD?

The Qur'anic appeal to rational thinking and enquiry is not restrained by the methodology of ijtihad. There is, in fact, no clear text on ijtihad in the Qur'an. Ijtihad as a concept originates in the hadith of the Prophet and the practice and precedent of the Companions. The methodology of ijtihad which is the basic theme of the science of the sources of law (i.e. *uṣūl al-fiqh*) is itself a product of ijtihad. It seems that the Prophet also saw ijtihad as a creative impulse rather than engaging in the technicalities of legal reasoning – as the *uṣūl al-fiqh* later developed in abundance. When the Prophet spoke of ijtihad or when he approved of its application, he seems to have done so in terms of ijtihad qua creative thinking.

One would readily admit that imposing restrictions on thinking, even if it were possible, by cultures and legal traditions could be exaggerated, in which case it would be prone to acquiring negative dimensions. One would not, on the other hand, advocate free thinking that is not limited by some kind of goal-orientation and values. Even the actual process of creative thinking, as earlier noted, is a skill that could be learned and refined by stages to direct it into productive avenues. The liberal tradition of the West tends to impose minimal restrictions on thinking whereas Islam tends to take a more guided approach to creative reasoning. Both the Islamic and Western traditions recognise the authority of reason as a criterion of judgment, yet the liberal tradition has, unlike Islam, isolated spirituality and faith from the ambit of scientific rationality.

However, the methodology of ijtihad was also influenced in the course of time by a variety of factors, including the political climate, the change of caliphate (*khīlafah*) to monarchy (*mulk*), Hellenistic thought in relationship to analogy (*qiyās*) and its syllogistic components, and the rift between the *ᶜulamā'* and ruling authorities.[67] *Uṣūl al-fiqh* and its proposed methodology followed a difficult course and became embroiled in technicality that had adverse consequences for ijtihad. What is needed now is to recapture the purity of this vital concept, to make ijtihad as our principal instrument for originality and healthy adjustment, but also to revise and reform some aspects of the theory of ijtihad itself that are no longer responsive to the prevailing conditions and challenges of our time.

I have elsewhere discussed the theory of ijtihad and its related issues and space here does not permit engagement in detail.[68] Yet I conclude this section by suggesting, however briefly, that the conventional theory of ijtihad needs to be revised and reformed in respect of the need 1) to recognise the validity of collective and consultative ijtihad (*ijtihād jamāᶜī*) side by side with that of ijtihad by individual scholars; and 2) to allow experts in other fields such as science, economics, and medicine to carry out ijtihad in their respective fields if they are equipped with adequate knowledge of the source evidence of Islam. They may alternatively sit together with, or seek advice from, those learned in Shariᶜah.

Ijtihad has in the past been often used as an instrument of diversity and disagreement rather than of unity and consensus. Although disagreement must admittedly be allowed in principle, yet there is a greater need today for unity and consensus. Scholars and learned bodies should not perhaps encourage excessive engagement in diversity of schools and sects but try to find ways that would help to close the gap between them and encourage unity on principles. This may require policy guidelines for different settings and countries, and, if so, that should be reflected in our approaches to ijtihad. Certain guidelines may also be provided by thinkers and leaders to stimulate consensus-oriented ijtihad within the ranks of the judiciary and legislative assemblies.

Ijtihad has in the past been conceived basically as a legal concept and methodology. Our understanding of the source evidence on ijtihad does not specify such a framework for ijtihad. Rather, we think of the original conception of ijtihad as a problem-solving formula for issues and challenges encountered by individual Muslims and the Muslim community. This would confirm our view of the need to broaden the scope of ijtihad to other disciplines beyond the framework of fiqh and *uṣūl al-fiqh*.[69]

According to a legal maxim of Islamic jurisprudence, there should be no ijtihad in the presence of a clear text of the Qur'an and hadith (*la ijtihād maᶜ al-naṣṣ*). This maxim should also be revised. This is because of the possibility that the text in question could now be seen in a different light and given a fresh interpretation in a different context. What we are saying is that the legal text may need to be understood first and that by itself may involve ijtihad. Hence ijtihad may not be precluded if it could advance a fresh understanding of the text in the first place.

The persistent decline of critical reason among Muslims is due partly to the notion that the exercise of personal judgment and ijtihad ceased with the epoch-making works of the legists and imams of the past. Added to this is the prevailing mindset that a Muslim should follow one or the other of the established schools of thought and abandon his judgment in favor of interpretations of the earlier centuries whose originators could have no conception of the necessities of the twenty-first century Muslims. Until about 1500 CE, independent ijtihad allowed Muslims and Muslim societies to continually adapt in the face of changing societal conditions and new advances in knowledge. Unfortunately, as Muslim civilisation began to weaken about four centuries ago in the face of Western advances, Muslims began to adopt a more conservative stance in an attempt to preserve traditional values and institutions. As a result, Muslim thinkers became inclined to view innovation and adaptation negatively. For all the rhetoric and symbolic form of the neo-radicals that tend to dominate the audience of Muslims, the spirit of Islam is often palpably missing from their endeavors, while more than ever ijtihad is needed where women, education, good governance and economic developments are concerned.

VI. POST ENLIGHTENMENT SECULARISM

Scientific rationality essentially reduces intelligence to the level of neural chemistry where mental and behavioral phenomena are understood merely as manifestations of physical processes. It tends to deprive man of his noblest dimensions (faith, love, beauty), separates the soul from the body, and the sensory from the intelligible. In the realm of economics, man is merely a producer and consumer of goods and is moved solely by his individual self-interest. This too is opposed to the Islamic viewpoint which sees in man morality and transcendent faith.

This physicalist analysis of intelligence is now increasingly being seen as conceptually inadequate. The real question is whether one may admit a human dimension which is autonomous and irreducible to a physical mass. In Moravia's phrase "can one posit something which exists and yet at the same time is non physical? Do the rejection of the soul and the achievements attained by bio and neurosciences oblige us to hold that man is nothing but body?"[70] Recently there have been attempts by some creative thinkers to reconceptualise notions of 'reason' and 'intelligence' along anti-materialistic lines drawing on the experience of older non-Western traditions, or even popular folk conceptions.[71]

Islamic philosophy – which mainly studies purposes, as against science which mainly studies causes – sees, in line with the Qur'anic teaching, the role of objects and events as signs of divine presence and action. Faith is understood by Muslims not as a limitation on science but as its vista for enrichment and perfection.[72]

The variant perspectives of Western philosophy and science are also behind the Western puzzlement why Muslims have not become more secularised. This unwarranted assumption has in the past led to mistaken assessments of Islam and continues to foster genuine misunderstanding concerning the real nature of Islamic religion and intellectual traditions. The misunderstanding is unfortunately not unique to Westerners. For the majority of Muslims today are also woefully uninformed of the depth and scope of their rich heritage on the authoritative validity of reason. Thinking

Muslims should work to vindicate the symbiotic relation of faith and reason in their religion and see it as a source of enrichment and contribution of Islam to human understanding and civilisation.

VII. CONCLUSION

This paper advanced a Qur'anic perspective on thinking, which in its critical and goal-oriented dimensions provides a set of guidelines that ensures its purity and purpose from negative reductionist influences. The guidelines so provided are also rich in advancing a spiritual dimension with the understanding that thinking which is not informed by morality and faith can lose its direction and purpose and can even become harmful to human welfare. From the Qur'anic vantage point the sciences of nature should be key to our cognition of the signs of God in the universe. For this may be instrumental in solving individual and social problems without interrupting the cosmic order and the human habitat on earth. The blatant disregard of ethical values in science has weakened scientists' sense of responsibility and contributed to the degradation of the human condition on the globe and brought unprecedented environmental degradation.

Since thinking is a skill that can be advanced by self-application and training, it is amenable to guidance, bereavement, and enrichment. Universities and institutions of learning in Muslim countries are generally short of resources, and those who have the means still fall short, to their detriment, of nurturing the culture of critical thinking, reading and research among their students and scholars. Centers of higher learning may do well to establish a new order of relationship between the natural sciences and humanities, and between all fields of knowledge and human welfare and also the avenues of benefit to society. The present-day education system is due for a reappraisal in order to instill creative thinking and breadth of vision among students and scholars that is informed by the interrelatedness of the various disciplines of learning. This could be done, as one observer suggested, "by adding sufficient number of courses in humanities to the science and engineering curricula, by cross-disciplinary interaction and collaboration."[73] The main characteristic of the human sciences, from the Islamic perspective, is that they are not value-free and have to be incorporated within the value system of Islam that is informed by the ethical and human dimension of values.

Semiotic content and tools cut across innumerable fields such as logic, linguistics, grammar, semantics, cognition, philosophy, anthropology, natural sciences, to name some. Work of Muslim scholars that falls nothing short of semiotic analysis in the strictest sense, could be highlighted and integrated into a common discourse. This is not far-fetched given that even 'Semiotics' as a comprehensive contemporary discipline, independent from philosophy and linguistics is in itself recent. 'Cognitive Semiotics' for example, a field that is attempting to mend the gap between science and the humanities, emerged only as late as in 1990s.[74]

It is ironic to note, however, that the vast majority of Muslims are wont to rote reading of the Qur'an which is patently vacuous and devoid of thinking. The Qur'an is usually read, committed to memory, and cited for its spiritual merit rather than intellectual stimulation and enrichment. This is evidently not the advice one obtains from the Qur'an itself. Al-Qaradawi has rightly observed about the current realities of public education in Muslim countries that "the system relies on memorisation and cramming more than it does on comprehension and analysis. A typical weakness of this method is that the memoriser forgets as soon as the exams are over. But if what is learned is founded in understanding and comprehension, its substance will remain in the mind and will not be prone to oblivion so quickly."[75] But the issue that we raise here is well-entrenched and originates in the overall emphasis that most educationists and jurists of earlier times have placed on the study of the Qur'an, hadith and fiqh manuals, often calling attention to words and sentences of the text at the expense of comprehension and analysis. The basic approach to Qur'an studies thus emphasised correct pronunciation and memorisation. This repetitive system of learning was particularly pronounced in the context of child education, although it was not confined to this framework as other and more advanced levels of Islamic scholarship also bore the same influence.[76]

Notwithstanding the profound influence of the Qur'an on the thoughts, mores, and cultures of Muslim individuals and societies, thinking by its nature does not lend itself to any predetermined framework and guideline. It seems that the Qur'an also seeks only to provide signs and signposts on thinking, but the subjective and innately individual bent of thinking is often inspired by imagination and insight which cannot be encapsulated by definitions and guidelines. A creative mind is unique by its attributes, and thinking that originates in a learned and upright individual is one of the greatest gifts of creation that can itself fit the description of divine example, or *āyah,* of God on earth.

It remains to be added though that imaginative thinking has also been sparkled by sources and influences among great thinkers of other cultures and traditions – just as we note also that the great thinkers of history emerged in all regions, cultures, and religions. The substance of these statements is upheld in a renowned hadith in which the Prophet instructed the Muslims to "seek knowledge, even unto China," and in another hadith that "wisdom is the lost property of the believer; he is entitled to it wherever he finds it." Knowledge and wisdom must therefore be ultimately seen as the shared achievements of humanity, endowed and posited by its outstanding and creative thinkers. This is also known from the fact that the outcomes of creative thinking are often shared and experienced far beyond geographical locales and frontiers – more so perhaps in the age of globalisation.

It is hoped that the great thinkers and leaders of humanity make it a part of their agenda and commitment to narrow down the distances and divide; between the intellectual and cultural traditions of the world and aspire them to the veritable vision of a shared destiny and wider human fraternity in their deliberations.

NOTES

1. See for details Elma Berisha, "The Qur'anic Semio-Ethics of Nature" in *Islam and Civilisational Renewal*, vol. 8, no.1 (January 2017), p.49f.
2. Ibid., p.51.
3. The rough equation that earlier Muslim scholars drew between the Islamic and Western conceptions of reason tended to be oblivious of the categories of reason and the Western critique of reason that divided it into "instrumental reason, critical reason, functional reason, abstract reason, imperialist reason, decentering reason" and the like. For details see Abdelwahab M. Elmessiri, "Features of the New Islamic Discourse," a Cairo conference paper, 1997.
4. *Sūrah Fuṣṣilat*, 41:53.
5. *Sūrah al-Dhāriyāt*, 51:20.
6. *Sūrah Ṣād*, 38:29.
7. Some commentators have distinguished a total of 30 expressions that revolve around thinking over the *ayāt*. See Abū Bakr al-Rāzī, *Tafsīr al-Kabīr* (Beirut: Dār al-Fikr), II, pp.222f.
8. *Sūrah Muḥammad*, 47:24.
9. Ian Richard Netton, *Allah Transcendent, Studies in the Structure and Semiotics of Islamic Philosophy, Theology and Cosmology* (London & New York: Routledge Taylor & Francis Group, 1989), p.321.
10. *Sūrah al-Baqarah*, 2:242.
11. *Sūrah Āl-ʿImrān*, 3:118.
12. Cf. Yusuf al-Qaradawi, *Al-ʿAql wa al-ʿIlm fī al-Qur'ān al-Karīm* (Cairo: Maktabah Wahbah, 1416/1996), p.36.
13. Al-Rāghib al-Iṣfahānī, *Mufradāt Alfāẓ al-Qur'ān* (Beirut: Dār al-Shāmiyyah, 1383/1964) under "Fikr".
14. *Sūrah al-Aʿrāf*, 7:175 and 176; see also *Sūrah al-Ḥashr*, 59:21; *Sūrah al-Rūm*, 30:21.
15. Cf., Karim Douglas Crow, "Islam and Reason" in *Al-Shajarah*, vol. 8, (2003), pp.120-1.
16. Abbas Mahmud al-Aqqad, *Al-Tafkīr Fariḍah Islāmiyyah* (Thinking is an

Islamic Obligation) quoted in Jamal Badi and Mustapha Tajdin, *Creative Thinking: An Islamic Perspective*, 2nd edn., (Kuala Lumpur: International Islamic University Malaysia, 2005), p.6.

17. Cf. Al-Qaradawi, *Al-ᶜAql wa al-ᶜIlm*, pp.41-45 quoting ibn Qayyim al-Jawziyyah's *Miftāḥ Dār al-Saᶜādah*, and Aqqad's book entitled *Al-Tafkīr Fariḍah Islāmiyyah* (Beirut: al-Maṭbaᶜah al-ᶜAṣriyyah, 1992).
18. *Sūrah al-Tawbah*, 9:122.
19. *Sūrah Āl-ᶜImrān*, 3:48.
20. cf. *Sūrah al-Jumᶜah*, 62:2, and passism.
21. *Sūrah al-Nisā'*, 4:54.
22. *Sūrah Luqmān*, 31:12.
23. *Sūrah al-Baqarah*, 2:269.
24. Cf. Al-Qaradawi, *Al-ᶜAql wa al-ᶜIlm*, p.200.
25. Cf. Ibid., p.202.
26. Al-Iṣfahānī, *Mufradāt Alfāẓ al-Qur'an*, p.249.
27. Sayyid Muhammad Husayn Tabataba'i, *Al-Mīzān fī Tafsīr al-Qur'ān* (Beirut: Al-Mu'assasah al-ᶜAlamī, 1383/1964), II, p.395.
28. Alauddin al-Mattaqi al-Hindi, *Kanz al-Ummah fī Sunan al-Aqwāl wa al-Afᶜāl* (Beirut: Mu'assasah al-Risālah, 1383/1981), hadith no. 5873.
29. Abū Ḥāmid Muḥammad al-Ghazālī, *Risālat al-Radd ᶜalā-Laduniyya*, ed., Abd Allah Riyad Mustafa, (Damascus: Dār al-Ḥikmah, 1986), p.241.
30. *Sūrah al-Naḥl*, 16:78.
31. Cf. Ahmad Fuad al-Ahwani, *Al-Tarbiyah fī al-Islām* (Cairo: Dār al-Maᶜārif bi-Miṣr, 1968), pp.227-228.
32. Cf. Aziz al-Azmeh, *Arabic Thought and Islamic Societies* (London: Groom Helm, 1986), p.109.
33. Cf. Diane F. Halpern, *Thought and Knowledge: An Introduction to Critical Thinking* (Mahwah: New Jersey, Lawrence Erlbaum and Associates, 1996), p.21.
34. Cf. Ibrahim B. Syed, "Critical Thinking" as online at http://www.lrfi.org/articles/articles_101_150/critical_thinking.htm.
35. Muhammad Iqbal, *The Reconstruction of Religious Thought in Islam* (Lahore: Shah Muhammad Ashraf, reprint 1982), p.127.
36. *Sūrah al-Ḥajj*, 22:46.
37. *Sūrah al-Naḥl*, 16:78.
38. *Sūrah al-Zumar*, 39:18.
39. *Sūrah al-Ḥāqqah*, 69:38-39.
40. Malek Bennabi, *Intāj al-Mustashriqīn* (Cairo: Maktabah ᶜĀmir, 1990), p.34.
41. *Sūrah Āl ᶜImrān*, 3:137.

42. *Sūrah Āl ʿImrān*, 3:140.
43. *Sūrah al-Aʿrāf*, 7:181–183.
44. Iqbal, *Reconstruction of Religious Thought*, p.139.
45. *Sūrah al-Ḥujurāt*, 49:6.
46. *Sūrah al-Zumar*, 39:6; *Sūrah al-Nisā'*, 4:1.
47. See for details Imam Feisal Abdul Rauf, *What's Right with Islam is What's Right with America* (San Francisco: Harper Collins, 2004), pp.4–5.
48. Georg W. H. Hegel, *Philosophy of History* (New York: Dove Books, 1956), p.109.
49. Louay Safi, "The Creative Mission of the Muslim Minorities in the West: Synthesizing the Ethos of Islam and Modernity," a conference paper presented at Westminster University, London, UK, February 21, 2004: http://lsinsight.org/articles/Current/MuslimMinorities.htm.
50. *Sūrah al-Jāthiyah*, 45:23.
51. *Sūrah al-Baqarah*, 2:120; see also *Sūrah al-Qaṣaṣ*,28:50; *Sūrah al-Kahf*, 18:28.
52. *Sūrah Yūnus*, 10:36.
53. *Sūrah al-Isrā'*, 17:36.
54. *Sūrah al-Najm*, 53:23.
55. Cf., M. H. Kamali, "Islam, Rationality and Science" in *Islam and Science*, (2003), vol. 1, no. 2, p.126f; see also Mehdi Golshani, "Philosophy of Science from the Qur'anic Perspective" in *Towards Islamisation of Disciplines* (Herndon: International Institute of Islamic Thought, 1989), p.73f.
56. *Sūrah Yūnus*, 10:32.
57. *Sūrah al-Anʿām*, 6:115.
58. *Sūrah al-Baqarah*, 2:170, see also *Sūrah al-Mā'idah*, 5:104.
59. *Sūrah al-Anbiyā'*, 21:54; *Sūrah al-Aʿrāf*, 7:71.
60. *Sūrah al-Aḥzāb*, 33:67.
61. *Sūrah al-ʿAnkabūt*, 29:39.
62. Cf. Ishfaq Ahmad, "Research and Development Culture in the Islamic World: Past and Present Problems and Future Directions" in Abu Bakr Abdul Majeed et al. (eds.) *New Knowledge, Research and Development in the Muslim World* (Kuala Lumpur: Institute of Islamic Understanding Malaysia, 2004), pp.14–15.
63. Ziauddin Sardar, *Islam, Postmodernism and Other Futures: A Ziauddin Sardar Reader* (London: Pluto Press, 2003).
64. Seyyed Hossein Nasr, *Traditional Islam in the Modern World* (Kegan Paul International: 1990).
65. See for a discussion Oliver Leaman, "Institutionalising Research and

Development Culture in the Islamic and Non-Islamic World: A Comparative Perspective" in Abu Bakr Majeed, (ed.) *New Knowledge*, pp.50–51.

66. Malek Bennabi, *Intāj al-Mustashriqīn*, p.26.
67. See for details Mohammad Hashim Kamali, "Issues in the Understanding of Jihad and Ijtihad" in *Islamic Studies*, 41 (2002), p.623ff.
68. There is a chapter on ijtihad in M. H. Kamali, *Principles of Islamic Jurisprudence*, 3rd edn., (Cambridge: Islamic Texts Society, 1991, 2003). See also my article "Issues in the Understanding of Jihad and Ijtihad" in *Islamic Studies*, 41 (2002), pp.617–635; and "Issues in the Legal Theory and Usul and Prospects for Reform" in *Islamic Studies*, 40 (2001), pp.1–21.
69. The present writer has advanced a new definition for ijtihad in his *Shari'ah Law: An Introduction* (Oxford: Oneworld Publications, 2008), p.165.
70. Sergio Moravia, *The Enigma of the Mind: The Mind-Body Problem in Contemporary Thought*, tr. S. Staton, (Cambridge: Cambridge University Press, 1995. First published in Rome, 1986), pp.4–5.
71. See for example, Howard Gardner, *Intelligence Refrained: Multiple Intelligence for the 21st Century* (New York: Basic Books, 1999).
72. See for details Roger Garudy, "The Balance Sheet of Western Philosophy in this Century" in *Towards Islamisation of Discipline*, (Herndon: International Institute of Islamic Thought, 1989), p.399f.
73. Mehdi Golshani, "From Knowledge to Wisdom: A Qur'anic Perspective" in *Islamic Studies*, 44 (2005), p.13.
74. See Martin Lings, "The Symbolism of the Letters of the Alphabet", in *A Sufi Saint of the Twentieth Century: Shaikh Ahmad al-Alawi: His Spiritual Heritage and Legacy* (Cambridge: Islamic Texts Society, 1993).
75. Yusuf al-Qaradawi, *Fiqh al-Awlawiyyāt*, p.68.
76. Cf., Al-Ahwani, *Al-Tarbiyah fī al-Islām*, p.189.